S0-AJQ-384

Mount St. Helens is an active volcano

Volcanoes

Aaron Frisch

A⁺

Smart Apple Media

COPYRIGHT

Published by Smart Apple Media

1980 Lookout Drive, North Mankato, MN 56003

Designed by Rita Marshall

Copyright © 2002 Smart Apple Media. International copyright reserved in all countries. No part of this book may be reproduced in any form without written permission from the publisher.

Printed in the United States of America

Photographs by Tom Stack & Associates (Bill Everitt, Dave Fleetham, Jeff Foott, Sharon Gerig, Mark Newman, Mike Severns, Spencer Swanger, Greg Vaughn)

Library of Congress Cataloging-in-Publication Data

Frisch, Aaron. Volcanoes / by Aaron Frisch. p. cm. — (Natural disasters series)

Includes index.

ISBN 1-58340-124-5

1. Volcanoes—Juvenile literature. [1. Volcanoes.] I. Title. II. Series.

QE521.3 .F76 2001   551.21–dc21   00-052646

First Edition 9 8 7 6 5 4 3 2 1

A Volcano Erupts

All around a tall mountain, the ground shakes slightly. The air gets warmer. Suddenly, the top of the mountain explodes. Black ash rises into the air, and red rivers of melted rock flow down the sides of the mountain. It's a volcano!

A volcano is a mountain with an opening that lets melted rock and hot gas escape from the earth. People have always been curious about volcanoes and are often terrified by them. In ancient Rome, it was thought that volcanic **eruptions** were

Lava can spew high into the air

caused by Vulcan, the god of fire. The word "volcano" comes from the name Vulcan. 〰 Volcanoes actually begin deep under the ground. Much of the middle of the earth is made of gas and melted rock called **magma**. Some of this gas and magma slowly rises through cracks in the ground. When the magma gets close to the surface of the earth, it col-

Since the 1400s, volcanic eruptions have killed about 200,000 people around the world.

lects in large pools called reservoirs. Then the magma gradu- ally melts a hole to the surface. This hole is called a vent. 〰 Volcanoes erupt when the magma and gas burst out of

the vent. Magma is called **lava** when it runs onto the surface

of the earth. Some lava is fluid and flows quickly. Other lava

may be sticky. Pieces of rock formed from sticky lava are called

Lava flowing into the sea creates hot steam

When volcanoes calm down, plants grow again

tephra. Tephra can also be dust, flakes of ash, or pieces of rock called volcanic bombs. Sometimes sticky lava plugs up a volcano's vent. This can cause the whole top of the volcano to blow up. Eruptions also blast a lot of gas into the air. Much of this gas is just very hot water called steam. Often the gas carries volcanic dust high into the air. When they are combined, gas and dust form a black smoke.

How Volcanoes Form

Most volcanoes form around the edge of the Pacific Ocean. Big plates of rocks move under the ground in this area.

This allows so much magma to rise to the surface that the area

is known as the "Ring of Fire." When magma breaks through

the ocean floor, underwater mountains are created. Some of

Volcanic eruptions can leave large craters

these mountains rise above the water and form **islands**. This

is how the Hawaiian Islands were formed. Volcanoes can

take different shapes. Some volcanoes are formed by lava that

pours out and spreads over a wide **Most volcanic bombs are about as big as a base-ball or basketball.**

area. The lava cools and turns into

hard rock. This gradually forms a low, **But huge ones can weigh almost 100 tons (91 t).**

dome-shaped volcano called a shield

volcano. Other volcanoes are formed as lava and tephra build

up around the vent. This forms tall, cone-shaped mountains

called composite volcanoes. Many of the world's most famous

volcanoes are composite volcanoes. These include Mount Fuji

in Japan and Mount St. Helens in the United States.

Shield volcanoes are formed as lava spreads

Volcano Groups

Scientists classify volcanoes into groups based on how often they erupt. Active volcanoes erupt a lot. Intermittent volcanoes may erupt only once a century.

Mount Vesuvius erupted in 79 A.D. in Italy. It completely buried the city of Pompeii in ash and lava.

Dormant volcanoes are "sleeping" volcanoes that have not erupted in a long time but may again someday. Extinct volcanoes have not erupted during human history and probably never will. It is impossible to stop a volcano from

This dormant volcano is now a forest

erupting. But scientists try to tell when eruptions will happen so people have time to get away. Volcanoes often give clues that they are ready to erupt. The sides of the volcano may bulge as the magma builds up inside. The rising magma may cause small **earthquakes**. And the temperature around the volcano may get warmer.

The Dangers of Volcanoes

Volcanoes can be very dangerous. The blasts from strong eruptions can destroy everything around the volcano

Volcanic eruptions can be spectacular to watch

for many miles. They may kill thousands of people and bury whole cities under ash and lava. Sometimes clouds of dust and ash rise into the sky and stay there for months. This can partially block the sun and even change the weather. Volcanoes are among nature's greatest displays of power. They have been shaping the earth for billions

Over time, volcanic ash that lands in farmers' fields makes the soil more fertile. This helps crops grow better.

of years. The more people know about volcanoes, the more safely they will be able to live near these fiery mountains.

Hawaii has many active volcanoes

Make Your Own Volcano

Most volcanoes are huge and take many years to form. But you can build your own volcano in just a few minutes.

What You Need

A large baking pan
Clay (brown or gray is best)
1/4 cup (60 ml) water
1/4 cup (60 ml) vinegar
One tablespoon (15 ml) baking soda
Red food coloring
Liquid dish soap

What You Do

1. Form the clay into the shape of a volcano in the baking pan.
2. Scoop out a small hole for the vent at the top of the volcano. If you wish, put a small container in the hole.
3. Pour the water into the hole or container. Stir in the baking soda, a few drops of red food coloring, and a few drops of dish soap.
4. To make the volcano erupt, pour in the vinegar. Watch as the red "lava" bubbles up out of the vent!

There are volcanoes on every continent on Earth

Index

Words to Know

earthquakes (URTH-kwakes)—shaking of the ground caused by the shifting of rock in the earth

eruptions (ee-RUP-shuns)—the breaking out of magma and gas from the earth

islands (EYE-lends)—small sections of land surrounded by water

lava (LAH-vuh)—hot, melted rock that flows onto the earth's surface

magma (MAG-muh)—hot, melted rock inside the earth

tephra (TEF-ruh)—pieces of rock blasted out of a volcano

Read More

Lye, Keith. *Volcanoes.* Austin, Tex.: Raintree Steck-Vaughn, 1996.

Murray, Peter. *Volcanoes.* Chanhassen, Minn.: Child's World, 1999.

Sipiera, Paul P. *Volcanoes.* New York: Children's Press, 1998.

Internet Sites

The Electronic Volcano
http://www.dartmouth.edu/~volcano/

Volcano World
http://volcano.und.nodak.edu/vw.html

Volcano Information Center
http://www.geol.ucsb.edu/~fisher/